Hollywood or Home

For Andrew and Eleanor Neilson — my stars

I can say without melodrama or malice that Hollywood ruined my life.
—Jerome Charyn

Hollywood or Home

Kathryn Gray

Seren is the book imprint of
Poetry Wales Press Ltd.
Suite 6, 4 Derwen Road, Bridgend, Wales, CF31 1LH
www.serenbooks.com
facebook.com/SerenBooks
twitter@SerenBooks

ISBN: 9781781727126
Ebook: 9781781727133

The publisher acknowledges the financial assistance of the Books Council of Wales.

Cover artwork: by Alain Magallon: 'Sunset Boulevard', oil on canvas.

Contents

Miramar

Ghost Rider—full throttle on my bike,
I fist-pump the sky as if I were not weary of jets—
jets being what I do—as if I still had *the need,*
the need for speed. It's true. I've lost that—
you know—that *certain* feeling. For somewhere
in this attenuated heart I know that Goose is
dead. He can no longer intercept. It is a familiar
script. Here in Fightertown near-permanent
sunset could give your average cinematographer
the perpetual boner. I do not know what I am
doing in Fightertown. Something vague yet
meaningful about my back story, all the baggage
explaining the arrogance I miss: my mother
spinning the one record over and over; my father
stained by ignominy, but accorded sufficient
mystery. And, of course, they, like Goose, are
dead. *You've got to let them go.* Tom Skerritt
said. Tom Skerritt told me that. Playing with
the boys—so ripped, so oiled—all I can think of is
bogeys like fireflies in the sky over Nam. Goose
is dead, but he was there. And Skerritt was
telling me. Skerritt said my father was a *natural*
heroic sonofabitch. I am better than him—and
worse. But Skerritt was slim on detail, so I am
none the wiser. *First one. I crashed and burned.*
I have the dog tags in my hand—how they hold
his heat. *Talk to me.* On set, Simpson is shouting,
demands more—well—anything—just more.
The problem is Val's hair. On deck, I stand before
the waves. Simpson was on set, but he, too, is
dead. I hold them in my hand. Faltermeyer's
'Memories' plaints. I stand before the waves.
I cast them out, out to the deep. But they are
corrode-resistant. We are looking at years.
Now the old number drops in the Wurlitzer.
The waves. *We had a love.* And Goose is still dead.

Hollywood

I have never gone to Hollywood.

I have never gone, but I would.

I have never walked a blistering dust road out from San Antonio.

I have never lunched at Spago.

I have never hitched to L.A. in my hick dress.

I have never shut my eyes, so tightly, *for this is sacrifice.*

I have never jumped from the H, but came close in the mind.

I have never signed_____.

I have never howled *MY PAIN* in the second-best bath of a mogul.

I have never been considered beautiful.

I have never warred with my sister for half a century.

I have never even *had* a sister, according to sources close to me.

I have never been forcibly removed from the Beverly Wilshire.

I have never sued the *National Enquirer.*

I have never heard—immortal—*YOU'LL NEVER WORK IN THIS TOWN AGAIN!*

I have never swum in champagne.

I have never licked the Walk of Fame.

I have never known a *has* from a *been.*

I have never.

Portrait of My Superego as Mommie Dearest

You've got to love her.
Her eyebrows are practically a fucking opera.

Fix me a vodka.

I do not want to think of cold cream,
so naturally I think of cold cream.
Cold cream.

She scatters the Vim,
and together we scour
the star system.

Even the roses must have it—
even the roses have it coming to them.
Everyone knows the truly
cultivated nurse a secret contempt
for beauty.

It's a question of fragility.

Or envy.

Though it hardly matters
either way when you're
the one swinging the axe, Mommie.

Why did you adopt me?

Cold, cold cream.

The wire hangers
sing their old song:
Something's Gotta Happen Soon.

Let us contemplate life turning
to nothing but bacteria before
our very eyes. Grim fur, grim fur.
On rare steak.
Eat! Eat! she says.

Whatever I did next,
I did for our own good.

Poor bitch.

I can tell you all this *now*, of course.
You can't libel the dead.

Meryl Streep is my therapist

I met a married man once, on a train. He was handsome.
He had the kind of face that made me think
of clean, smooth hands. I should add that
in the end nothing really happened.

I have done terrible things I will not own.

The dingo took my baby!

Bear with me.

Men have left me. No Vietnam. They simply went.
You must hear this sort of thing all the time. But.
I have stood, hooded, on the jetty;
the sea—the sea turned over my mind, roughly.

I have been very 'tired and emotional'.
I cannot afford a rehab facility.

There are not enough Key lime pies in this world
for all the people who deserve them. In the face.
Yes, this is heartburn.
You might be onto something.

O Michael! O Michael! O Michael!

I worry that I'm all cliché.
I like to fake accents with strangers.
I suppose that tells you a lot.

I suffer from Imposter Syndrome. Or maybe not.

I had a farm—

Six Ways of Looking at John Cazale

I

John's eyes—the tender inquisition.
You are not, in fact, looking at *him*.

II

In makeup, John wears Fredo's face,
looks in the mirror, thinks,
I can do something with this.

III

John dropping a gun with conviction,
unconvincingly. Inimitable.

IV

John blinking out
from the afterlife
in disbelief
when you bring up his name
in the conversation.

V

John rising from his bar stool, singing.
*I wanna hold you
so much—*

VI

Wyoming.

Bill Hicks Impossible Love Poem

What freight passed between us.
Such sorrow in our final cigarette.

I shared my dream of you, alive again;
you shared your view of me:

Honey, now you're sucking on the tailpipe
of mediocrity. But pity thickened

in your eyes and, in pity for myself,
I slipped a hand under your trench

to touch you at the tender place.
Does it hurt? Does it hurt still, even so?

Bill, you would give nothing away.
Are you afraid? Are you afraid yet?

A Bandana

I'll say, like some, you wore it for the wound
—Sweet tourniquet of youth!

Or how you might have hammed it up for war
with the morning mirror.

(Let me gesture
for you now: two fingers
                          together,
The Deer Hunter.)

I've read how once you'd determined to bind
the hose to tailpipe, failed;

found out. (Imagine the sum of years:
Not even a fucking
                          bandana
sincere.)

While most aver—its proper use—
the staunch against hyperhidrosis,

perhaps, (no irony!) as you said,

in truth, real truth,
it was that thing   that thing,
that kept your head,

that thing

from
exploding.

Shermerverse

1. John in Darkness

The wrong side of the tracks,
little houses in their yearning
abandonment—

where Andie, in dreams,
is troubled by the notion
she is, in fact, an elaborate fiction—

and Bender turns in fists,
denying his creator, even
at this late hour—

and over town, Cameron
and Ferris at last are levelled
by the inkling of an ending—

and Allison mouths to black
the complaint:
she was underwritten—

left to their own devices,
Meadowbrook and Shermer High
are monuments of *no more*—

only Carl, night-shifting, knows
the answer to *whatever will we do
when we grow up*—

2. Regarding Your Day Off

Cameron—find this love letter, thirty years hence, for your face is the very architecture of loneliness. I will tell you what my *carpe diem* might have been: to stand in a museum with you, considering Seurat, while our twinned hearts beat with inconsequence. Or rewind to the tower, our crowns against the glass... But, then again—what good, for people like us, of either view? (And anyway this is all about *you*.) We could stay in bed all our lives, tending each other's injury so exquisitely. O, o needy bonsai! But today is a sunny day, and so we might partake of the fictional pool I've constructed in the mind, and you could play at suicide, and your fake drowning will be genius! We two are connoisseurs of the sick joke. Cameron, a reminder that your dead father has it coming, so feel no remorse when we fuck up his car. As for whatever comes after? We could laugh and point at Ferris, the Sausage King long since run to fat. Perhaps he doesn't even *exist*. You know, he hates that. And life is bad enough without friends who make you feel worse. *Danke Schoen.*

3. The Duckies, in their mid-life

Though large on soul,
we always lacked a certain something.

Kristy Swanson was a bait-and-switch,
in retrospect. The ultimate.

It spikes the existential cry:
What happened to the script?

Our Maker's room thickens
with the 'deep' stuff. It is not tenderness.

The sucker gets no succour in this world—
or so some guy must once have said.

Michael McIntyre is worth 50 million dollars

Look at my life—control pants and all these undone plans.
I don't want to go into the 'emotional baggage',
but today I read that Michael McIntyre is worth 50 million
dollars; you might well imagine what this knowledge
did to me. Yes, I was weeping and shaking and raging—
and weep-raging in between the shaking. But Michael
McIntyre has the face of a good man who is entirely
confident of his goodness. So there's some comfort in
that. I've no reason to believe he is less than deserving;
at least, in respect of the fact that the *good* deserve *things*,
and I am *not good*, even if it's true that I have stood
in the coldest rooms, opening up a vein or two, before
audiences of nine—or fewer! But then, some bastard's
always got there first, or—worse—their veins are *bigger*.
These days I am nothing but this—this—
sack of regret in control pants. Even sacks of regret
need control pants; in fact, they need them more than
most. This is how life tends to happen: you plane at your
soul for the wrong art, and end up with the shavings, unless
you're Michael McIntyre. A sack of shavings. So you're
pretty much average, unless you take it too much to heart.
A man I loved once told me I was the funniest woman he'd
ever met—and he didn't even drink. Perhaps I should have
taken time to probe that. You've got to make your peace.
Michael McIntyre seems like a good man. I wonder if he is

As told by Alan Smithee

So I was getting an enema somewhere off Ventura... All things considered, it had been a rough year. I had recently experienced severe complications following an operation for a septal perforation. Earlier, in April—after another futile round of creative battles, and wanting to make my point more clearly—I'd misjudged the drop from a second-floor balcony of the Beverly Wilshire, suffering such devastating fractures, I was now, by all accounts, 'a walking miracle'. Hence: the pills. But life was not yet finished with me. Chronic pinkeye was a monthly torment, while mysterious styes simply aggregated... The portents were everywhere. 'A broken man of no vision', according to *Variety*, and, besides, much reduced in circumstance: nothing but six flat-screens from the settlement for company; jerking off wildly, nightly, to the *Heaven's Gate* audio playing out in unison in every room of my otherwise unfurnished rented condo... So, yeah, I was in need of cleansing... Jesus—the annals. It took me back to film school. Primordial flora... The glorious mess of youth... Hell, the truth in my guts spoke to that bucket. I was crying. You know, real *ugly* crying. Rock bottom. The bottom of the rock... Until the earth itself slipped away... All the Alan Smithees of time stood before me, their faces etched with the tragic history of losers' integrity: botched prenups under California law, the serial myocardial infarctions, the star vehicles, you name it... From this throng stepped Michael Cimino. *Never forget these words, whatever the cost*, he said of the words I can't remember now. Waking in Cedars-Sinai, I resolved to change my life. I opened my eyes for a sign through the blur. She lightly brushed my covers and is now my fourth wife.

Away with the birds

Away with the birds! I was away.
Or so they said. But, ah! In truth,
the mind was a nineteenth-century
valetudinarian—chairbound,
earthbound—beholding the garden
in which the seasons played
their part remorselessly. I watched
the birds with no time for me.
Away they went. And although they
did not love me and had, no doubt,
better places to be, I grieved for
my birds. Such is the quality of desire.
And although I rail at others' dreams,
I must tell you of the night a man
came to me and presented a plate
on which all good things were laid.
O, my friends—for once, I ate.
And what was left was this gift:
the figure of a small bird, so artlessly
rendered I could hear its bounding heart.

The Portable Dorothy Parker

Morning comes at you like a gun:
point blank. That's what you get for shots,
dear heart. That's what you get for wanting *more*.
In retrospect, you'd have it all un-poured now, you would—set back in
   the cabinet
instead of your damned blood.
But that's regret for you. *Duh*. Times like this you think of her.

Yeah, you think of her.
Parker. Sure you do. And you think of a *literal* gun.
O Blood-
shot
Martyr of the Jäger before the bathroom cabinet!
As usual, it is only in your time of *extremis* that you realise more

Ibuprofen is needed. Alas. And woe. That need for more—
denied—is always quietly heartbreaking, isn't it? Her
face is on your mind, but really it's merely the cabinet's
mirror as you close it, quietly. That's all. You're not gone.
You're not even close to gone, though you heard a shot
in the mind and feel your blood—

well, *figuratively speaking*, it's blood—
slosh around your ankles like the water from that pipe last August. (More
cost!) At least you're giving it one more shot.
At least *that*. No one would blame you if you gave up. Not even her.
Not even your friends, but a number of your friends have gone.
They have been 'disappeared', perhaps. The mind is a terrible cabinet,

populated by indescribable figurines. The cabinet
peers into you. It offers no explanation—it's a *cabinet*, for chrissakes!—
   but you must infer that blood
is what's required from you now. 'Artistic commitment'. Anyway, you
   were thinking of *Sunset Gun*

just the other day, and of course you're thinking of Parker now, too, as
   you channel-hop to *Gilmore*
Girls. Incredibly, Rory is reading *The Portable Dorothy Parker*.
That's long-shot

odds coming in *just for you*. Synchronicity, practically. It makes you want
   to give it another shot,
in fact. But *really now*. This is the year. So of course you surf the net
until three in the afternoon. It would be a pity to waste this hangover.
It's not malingering, not actually. Research in service of ideas for my
   imagined poem of Parker. I call this the 'blood
test'. But facts always bring me grief. When I love someone, I love them
   more
than they want to be loved. If they weren't dead already, they'd sleep
   with a gun.

I don't want to think about a gun, but I often do. I don't want to think
   about O'Dwyer's
office—heaving blood-red in that New York sunset—in which stood
   the filing cabinet
where who knows how many shot glasses' worth of her ashes, exactly,
   were kept for seventeen years before finally coming to rest in—of all
   places—Baltimore.

Fresh Hell

There are men in small, unkind rooms, lit by naked bulb. They know fresh hell.

Fresh hell is a war on. Everywhere. I know because—pictures.

People are getting very angry these days.

So today I bought a new dress. Here is a picture.

I want to put EVERYTHING IN CAPS LIKE CHER.

Why can't life be EVERYTHING IN CAPS LIKE CHER?

I want to be a star. I'd die for my art. But I worry no one would care.

Small, unkind rooms. My unkind room is so small. A naked bulb in the mind, swinging.

I have a book out. My book has been out for sixteen years. Sixteen long years.

That's before most of you existed. Before fresh hell, even. Unimaginable.

But I am very relevant. Look at these abominable faces. That's mine.

It's mine, but I like it. From a certain angle it is actually quite kind. Or has semblance of being.

It's true I cannot locate Syria on a map, but here is Syria. This is a picture.

That's somewhere in Syria. Fresh hell. With feeling. There are angry men. Men are typing.

Women are typing things also. People are typing the fresh hell out of other people.

I am pinned. Or, my glory is pinned. Pinned butterfly. A pinned butterfly cannot fly.

But a pinned butterfly is fresh hell (beta). That's what a pinned butterfly is, surely.

A pinned butterfly, in a cabinet, in a small, unkind room. Look at it, by naked bulb.

Kanye would. Kanye knows art. Kanye knows true art is fresh hell.

What's happening? That is happening. It is very more fresh. It is very more of the now.

It is collapsing. Were there people in the building?

Fuck butterflies, pinned or otherwise. I always want more more more.

I am collapsing in a small, unkind room. Is it yours?

Donald

Donald is unhappy today.
Donald is unhappy in the familiar way.
Donald looks in the mirror, checks out Donald.
Donald queries, *Donald?*
Donald knows he's not the man they say he is.
Donald has been reading Camus lately.
Donald is fingering Vaseline between the absurd walls, religiously.
Donald suspects this isn't helping.
Donald goes to the men's room.
Donald is unshackled.
Donald thinks, *It must have been the Waldorf salad.*
Donald is off the cuff.
Donald likes golf.
Donald likes pussy.
Donald knows what Donald likes.
Donald would like to get off this bus.
Donald likes golf.
Donald wants to drive a golf cart, no hands!
Donald is feeling the imaginary wind in his alleged surgical graft.
Donald remembers simpler times.
Donald doesn't need permission.
Donald was there.
Donald was interviewed by Oprah in 1988.
Donald never said he was a saint.
Donald is getting hungry.
Donald says, *I just want to be me.*
Donald is unhappy.
Donald is wanting a big steak sandwich.
Donald hollers, 'Order the biggest fucking steak sandwich they've got!'
Donald knows he likes golf.
Donald is certain of that.
Donald is not the man they say he is.
Donald is a man of the people.
Donald said this.
Donald wonders sometimes if someone else said this.
Donald denies it.
Donald likes Cheez Whiz.
Donald is a feminist.
Donald's favourite films include *Beaches* and *Terms of Endearment*.

Donald never gets the chance to share like that.
Donald took a married woman furniture shopping.
Donald is going to incarcerate Hillary Clinton.
Donald is going to build a big wall.
Donald ponders his absurd walls.
Donald considers the ineffable mystery of the Waldorf salad.
Donald likes Scotland.
Donald likes golf.
Donald likes Donald.
Donald would like to turn Scotland into a golf course.
Donald is unhappy.
Donald likes doing things with his hands.
Donald demands, 'Look at those hands—are they small hands?'
Donald knows it's a man's prerogative to have dreams.

Nineteen-seventy-something

Everyone was kissing you at parties—
and *look at how you've grown!*
There were uncles, everywhere.
There was never any shortage of uncles.
Wherever did they all come from?
Yearning for adulthood, its mysteries,
was staring out the test card on
the Ferguson. There was a man you
recall who lived at the turn of the lane,
and you had to be very careful of him,
but you never thought to ask why,
or perhaps you had wanted to ask, but
somehow could not. Looking back,
maybe you made that one up. Everyone
knows his name. Everyone was
pinching your cheeks. Everyone was
there, standing on a loud, endless carpet.
Kissing you at parties. You can see
them there—being harmless. You
are sitting on the stairs. You are lying
in front of the Ferguson, staring out
the test card. It's been going on forever.
Nothing lasts. Everything lasts forever.
All your aunties are in the kitchen.
So many aunties! They have stopped
talking. They are smiling down at you,
forever. There is never anything to watch
on the Ferguson, even when there is.
Men in kipper ties have their hands
up things. They are smiling at you, kindly,
from the Ferguson. You know you are
safe as the houses on the quiet close,
but still you wonder how the men
in kipper ties came to do the things
they did. None of your uncles did things
like that, or perhaps they did, but you
didn't know about it. Or maybe in
their dreams they are sitting with a bird
on their knee, and the bird is talking

to them, and the voice is their own.
Maybe in their dreams that is their job.
And you wonder when you see them at
the parties, and everyone is kissing you.
Maybe when you grow up you will write
better things than the Friday evenings
on the Ferguson when comedy value
was someone walking into a room,
their Coke-bottle glasses held
together with an Elastoplast Airstrip.

Brundibár

You are innocent.
To watch, merely, is not to be complicit—
at least, surely, not from such distance.

Yet still the ache in you, the sheer insistence
that has to know:
And did the children, then, believe their song?

You want to believe it so.
You are, after all, a good person.
And you have, no doubt, great sentiment.

But Gerron's dilemma—
its efficiencies of horror—
will always prove you wrong.

KCN

A man protests his innocence in the third person
before drinking from the vial of poison
live on your television.
       Someday, you might begin,
It was the day without birdsong... forgetting
the day you first heard of the village of Stupni Do,
in the vague municipality of Vareš – the facts
of which, even now, stand contested. Before this,
you were thinking on *else* – where or things:
longings, perhaps, or decisions to be making.
We are only human, too human.
We have our private longings.
We have our decisions to be making.
Good men summon the doctor.
A man succumbs to cerebral hypoxia.
Or perhaps you never heard of Stupni Do, after
all. But still, *It was the day without birdsong.*
Perhaps you never heard of the vegetable pit,
or the women. You never heard about any of it.
Nonetheless, what that village knows –
remote, arcane – is what the blood shows:
anything can happen anywhere,
so long as the will is there.
The stories of the empty air of aftermaths
are groundless, utterly groundless. In Stupni Do,
in the vague municipality of Vareš, the little,
blameless birds call and answer, answer and call.

Hotel
Cecil
LOW
DAILY
WEEKLY
RATES
700 ROOMS

This monument to profit and loss,
conceived by Hanner, Dix, and Schops.

The Beaux Arts turn night terrors
for sailors, for lovers, for all my Dahlias.

By gun, by noose, by blade, or by poison.
The fracture in the Main.

The Bloody Mary I sink in the bar.
The spasming mirrors of the elevator.

A faucet I turn, which never runs clean.
This, this is not my dream.

I am the world's last barman poet

Let me tell you: staying relevant

in 'volatile times' is no mean feat.
And where I shake, it's still 1988.

Hippy hippy slake.
Behold: the Earthquake.

Bad taste?
This Irish Car Bomb, for instance?

Don't take me so *literally*.
I know my history

from a shot
glass. And I'll stir what I want.

The 20th Century
is getting old. Even the Kamikaze

has had its day. And as for
the Cosmopolitan—someone order

a Corpse Reviver? I like a girl
with balls.

Death in the Afternoon.
The Four Horsemen.

Now you're talking.

Coughlin's Law #127

So basically, son, it all comes down
to misdirection.
Up go the bottles in the air.
Odds are
the poor bugger's
not flairing, but flailing.
But you can bet the bastards
will see what they *think* is there.
Christ, they'll even cry out for *more*.

Cold Open

The woman at the station betrays nothing.
There is no cause for alarm. You are
in the grip of the season, only. But
still you cannot stop yourself from looking
and wondering what it all means if it
means nothing. That woman is too casual.
It must mean something. Her face upturns
to the camera, and the word slips from you
—*devastating*—and the people are looking.
Years later, you begin again, itchy paranoiac
that you are, for the hundredth time
at least believing yourself to be believing
yourself to be writing yourself down.

Bournemouth

The sea tonight—so comported—
is no threat. Let us walk along the front.
Let us ponder the Flood,
my imaginary friend. We've been,

so far, so scrupulous—yet what
comes of it? But the sea itself is innocent.
And the front, too—utterly benign.
Place your hand in mine,

for I am afraid of my own mind.
How it turns. How it folds itself
over and over—O my endless, sentient
serviette! It will not hold water,

the doctor said. And I don't do God.
Forgive me, Mrs Lightband. I am
lost—even if this proven, human fact.
And I want only to walk with you,

as each star bleeds so long, and breaks
to each final point. And my tears
will be nothing new, and the stars—
our startlers—the stars impossibly accrue.

High-concept

So there's this woman—
—there's this woman,
right?
Picture it.

Going mad.
And I mean BLANCHE mad.
Wearing 'the face of dread',
like this: .

She's into films,
you know,
and yeah, yeah, *icons*—
like, *really iconic* stuff...

She's the butt of every joke
in the office...
We're looking for
a young Sissy Spacek.

It's 'relatable'.
It's really 'relatable' stuff.
Principal themes:
'Urban Alienation'

and 'Dreams'...
We'll signal this
with, say, close-ups
of high heels

spiking rain... Just one idea. Anyway.
She buys her lonely groceries.
She masturbates
to the *National Enquirer*.

Saddest thing ever.
But mostly
we watch her
at the late-night screenings...

Tension builds…
Absolutely *nothing*
happening…
Until.

Her thirty-third viewing
of *The Purple Rose of Cairo*—
Bobby knows some guy
over in Rights at Metro—

and she walks out to a score
deranged
between Carpenter
and Horner…

And meaning is everywhere.
She turns the key
of her apartment door.
We know what she'll find.

We know she's going mad.
Evicted from her own mind
by love.
Or so we think.

But here comes the money shot.
We fade to black.
For. Eternity.
See?

This is still at the concept
stage, but subject to finance—
we're calling it [pause and flourish]—
Sincerities.

Handsome Weeping Boy

I cannot cry.
I have need of a handsome weeping boy.

Handsome weeping boy. His tears are
pear cultured pearls against his cheeks;

he is in touch with his emotions; he
leaks. Strap me to a chair.

Freeze-frame the oxygen tank
in *Beaches*. These days it is so hard to be

authentic. Handsome weeping boy,
I hear you. Your shoulders move beside me

so gently—breeze caught by a tree!
Debra Winger is dying again.

Handsome weeping boy, with your
handkerchief to stem the flow. *The feels*

is what the kids call it now, and I— I am
so full, I am running on empty.

I cannot cry.
I have need of a handsome weeping boy.

The Meet–Cute

Of course, a rain will come, the kind you've known,
which you choose to interpret as a miracle. How
large rain renders gutters elaborate; their fretwork
fugitive, an offering to the lost and low of this world.

There must be a girl—a girl in a cloche hat. The hat
will be the colour of a hot blush as hands fly to
meet cheeks and lips O to the suddenness of it all.
And this we determine behind the black and white.

It will be New York. And we may infer that the girl
is late for some as yet inscrutable but crucial prior
engagement which will never occur. Overcoats
and fedoras move the crowd. She has no umbrella.

The little cloche hat bleeds crimson, and stockings
darken, and she will shoulder through for shelter
under an awning. She may be a secretary or perhaps
a fragrant stenographer. She lives with a loud mother.

She checks her watch, when the smallest drop from
the awning's edge turns time into an enormous tear.
It is hopeless. Across the city, the flower sellers bring
in their wares, wet roses proving frail things heavy.

And what of the young man who stands next to her?
Their faces are the mise-en-scène of a missed coincidence.
Somewhere, blocks down, a café with two empty chairs.
It will not be now. And the rain, as you know, stops.

Meta

ways to be   not be   with you   are infinite
though some involve a dress   a yellow dress   though it
can hardly be considered the principal culprit   but
of course it is
         it is entirely to blame   and your eyes   are   kind
for once   or maybe the yellow dress,   yes ,
it's just the yellow dress
     and your hands so sincere
         don't make me think of this   please don't
but circumstance and you were somewhere   else
a building collapsed and I was standing there
         waiting   innocent   in my yellow dress
as arranged   it took them weeks to find my body   weeks
         and though you never knew me   you read about it
  somewhere   and were crying   inexplicably
in front of your sudden wife and children
         or there was no harm done   after all
                         I stood clear
and you were gently, so gently   explaining instead   sorry
not sorry   *Look, this thing can't happen   We must never meet
again*   and I was listening   and I never do that, always
                 almost never   so no harm done   or
     there was no yellow dress   but even absence is
significant   you of all people know this   I was
     watching a woman in a yellow dress
yes, among the pleats were layers of hidden meaning   but
that was just a film   and films mean   absolutely nothing,
virtually speaking   darling   to think of it is dizzying dizzying
         I tell you   la la
         that's how I go in my yellow dress   I never owned
a yellow dress   in my life   I have a thousand yellow dresses   or
     maybe more   that's what I sing   that's where I go to
         and when I buy the yellow roses   and am happy on
     the bright street   the part of me who never knew you
wishes   all the same   you would accept it   how she
wishes you would   why can't you stop
reminding her

that she never met you   whenever she sees
a woman in a yellow dress   or holds the roses
     or is doing nothing in particular
it's the only way you know how to love   I suppose
turning everything meta

Lovely Young Men

You get to forty-eight—suddenly—and everywhere—
the lovely young men. You cannot even stand on
a bus without some lovely young man. You cannot
even lie back in the chair with your mouth of horror
and be at peace with your diminishment a moment
longer: you have reached that certain age when even
your dentist is the lovely young man now. Truly,
they are everywhere you look. And it is appalling—
their beauty. Each moment so corrupted! When
they hand you your change at Starbucks, for example,
you ought to be ashamed—and you are, *unashamedly*—
since all you can think of is their unbridled cock,
which tragically makes an exception for you, and what
this thought does will push you to concentrate
—*so hard*—just to bring forth your name when they ask,
and when they spell it incorrectly on the cup,
a little part of you dies the more—if such is possible—
but you don't care, because you are thinking of their
cock, and of what that thought does to you. Incredible.
Even out walking with your mother-in-law, there is no
escape, for the perfect buttocks of a lovely young man
come into view, and you wonder if she sees them too,
and if they would make her life complete, but it
would be so awkward to enquire. Why do they smell
so good? And how do they know to wear *that* shirt?
Look at the way they smile at you, not knowing they
know exactly what you need them to do. Their faces
are light—so very little has happened to them yet.
And the way they run their fingers through their hair,
casting you out—again and again and again—from
paradise… Is there any pleasure in sorrow quite like it?
A lovely young man hooks a thumb into his belt, talks
you through his PowerPoint. And it is getting so hot
in the meeting room. And it occurs to you how strange
that you think only of their cocks, or all that their
bodies and faces promise of cock, when as a solemn girl
all you cared about, really, was their hearts, and when
you weep that night for the life unlived, which you do,
you are never sure whom it is exactly you are weeping for.

Bruce the Shark

Like all the nice girls, I love a polyurethane shark.
When you do that thing with sharky-shark eyes—
deep, so deep as an emptied ocean—all I can say is,
it's fortunate you're wipe-clean.

I can hardly stand it.

I come over pure Quint.

People warned me. People said, *with a snout
like that, he's your textbook emotional avoidant.*

But what to do, when I'm sexy for pneumatics
under the skin? Those levers banging and crashing
like the beds in some imagined B&B in Hartlepool,
just so your tail can do *this!*

And when your mouth opens and closes with not
so much more than a fart and a wheeze,
and you don't actually speak…

What were you thinking?

That question is rhetorical.

Action is character.

Those chompers going up and down!
And my legs, my legs! Dear GOD.
Now I'm in two.
You really know what to do to a girl.

It has been so many years, but still I play it out
in my off-hours. Here is the girl, on a lilo;
her loosed hair trails in the amenable waters
off Amity Island. What could possibly go wrong?

Funny, I know—I cannot quite recall your name now.

I *think* it was Bruce.

But anyway—there's more than one of you.

Some fragment

So many years now!
Time—the great *annealer.*

And I—I am resilience,
if nothing else.

Listen how it plays
on the stereo:

that man knows
I don't like you, but I love you

Night and Day, 1957

No one is immune.
Imagine Sinatra and the gun.
The mattress with its bullet holes
become art: the human soul.

Our hearts are stubborn—
as when we listen,
years later,
when it's finally, truly over:

our future both the mourned
and the mourner
of itself; the future
no longer exists, and never did.

Nelson Riddle strikes up
his orchestra,
and Sinatra opens
another vein for Ava Gardner.

Slightly, a Lost Boy

Not that my heart is a stopped clock.
Not that I even think of it at all,
come to think of it. To tell the truth,
I've long since regarded such things
as more or less inevitable, particularly
at three in the morning. There is,
quite naturally, the perambulator
to consider, and the smallness of you
tumbling out of time so long ago,
it might as well have been yesterday,
for what that means… That sort
of set-up can make you emotional.
But my ways are logic, lately. I tell
myself you are happy with your gift.
I see you, *there*—much pleasure in
your flute, fashioned from a branch,
and you are dancing! Dancing to your
self! You are merry, and you are
grateful for that tree. I don't think
you are lonely, not especially.
Truly—I don't. You have company.
I don't think you give much thought
to it, quite honestly. Still, I ponder
the story, its radical departure. Maybe
someone is sleeping on the job. I've
thought of that. A lacuna in my heart,
this morning night. The boys stay lost,
but not really, not really when you
come to think of it, which mostly I do
not. It's just that it's three in the night
of morning, and I do that hauntological
thing with the pages. I guess this is
what happens when you get to my age.
Not that I miss you. Not even, Slightly.

Love

after Douglas Sirk

Take me to the country club in my red dress.
Make me locally infamous.

Fix me a Martini—*Dry*—
I am getting weepy. I almost want to *die.*

O take me, please, to the clinic in Zurich.
I'm not being *ironic*—

I cannot see to see!
You—you have blinded me!

Be my gardener,
and I can make the moves like Lana Turner:

look what my eyeballs are doing now!
This is all that heaven allows,

and then some (uh, OK, that's Jane Wyman).
Don't say I am, I am a poor imitation—

O, you. Magnificent. Obsession.

Two Small Erotic Scenes from Imagined New York, with Food

1. Warm Rolls

I am thinking of that small place that nobody knows
but the cognoscenti. After all these years

it's nothing short of a miracle it's still in business—
requiring, as it does, such specific conditions

for existence; you've joked about it often enough:
the early hours, a hard rain's aftermath. See how

the lights come on? *See?* Appointed now,
and stubborn as ever—like the heart. But when

you hold one in your palm, and when you bite,
you'll understand that miracle again. This is

the world nobody knows, outside of the films—
nobody but us. So will you rise now, please rise!

For the warm rolls?

For the warm rolls are the most perfect of all.

2. Oyster Pail

How am I supposed to focus on the case—
the storyboard of time and place—
when you are pulling always deeper from the pail
with your legalese and chopsticks?
Impossible.
There's something between us,
you must admit.
Something I can't quite solicit,
but divine by the noodles

you'll press to your lips—
(and yes, they *are*)—all lubricious
flourish. You and your distraction techniques!
I love the way you send me home with longing.
'We've got an early start in the morning.'

Durante

So I 'loved' some guy in an alley in Rome.
OK—it was hardly *Three Coins in the Fountain*.
I only knew his first name.
But times like this don't roll around again
in a millennium. I was fresh from the train;

he was there on business. By chance
we both found ourselves in the Café de Paris.
Romance
was not on the agenda. Neither of us
was looking for commitment. Your average *lust*?

Certamente no. We *saw* each other,
that *truth* of what we were made for.
You know how it is: he has his papers;
you're wearing the red linen dress. Whatever
happens next is inevitable. You leave together

in the fullest silence. Practically unbearable.
And then he has you up against the wall,
and is driving it home as much as he is able.
You've never been more available.
The little church sounded three bells.

I heard him cry
her name and wept hot tears from my thighs.
When I tell you I could have died
happily there and then—no word of a lie.
We never even said goodbye.

Every once in a while I fondle the memory
of his *amore*. She comes to me—like poetry!

Quellenstraße, 1100

February—and I was young.
Spring Street! My blue bag was swinging

in uncommon warmth, even the shadowed
shapes of pavement under awnings

seemed ripe with a peculiar kindness
and promise. The snows, at last, had gone,

and this new street was my own.
I was so small, walking the street

in casual desire and joy. *Linden! Linden!*
the heart wants to cry,

and end it there.
But that would be a happy fiction.

Then, I did not know
how far I would have to go, how long alone;

not even when I came upon the febrile
water from that fractured main

—tableau of wonder in such sun,
merely. Two nuns

stood smiling in their placid certainties.
Spring Street again!

I have thought about it often down
the years, not that in the grand scheme

any of this matters. Too much has
happened since. Why do we remember

what we remember? How do we know
what makes us keep notice, waiting

on the things I no longer believe in—
immanence, for one—holding me

so tenderly now in that February day,
when I was young?

Watermelons

I carried a—I did—I carried a—watermelon
or two in my time. Truth told, I wanted nothing
more than to dance. Boys can teach you that,
but first you must master the watermelon.

In dreams, you come to me again, wielding
the syringe charged with Stolichnaya; I present
your patient, the watermelon; now precision,
now sorrow—your eyes as ever the consultant

anaesthetist's. O love, O loss, O blasphemy!
I will have you say: *Do this in remembrance of me.*

Chrysanthemums

The chrysanthemums—so very stubborn.
Yellow chrysanthemums! I have them

on the brain these days. Late summer is
always memory—so promiscuous with us—

and which garden now impossible to tell—
but the yellow chrysanthemums still

are here—O failings—my failings of—
where once you stood and were.

On Listening to the Carter Family's 'My Old Cottage Home'

O blue—so blue—
the grass I've walked in—

thinking always on you,
my sweet ghosts.

Those were the years
when gladly

I would have been
your prodigal,

but for a home, a key—
and O, you absent hosts!

How to tell
now of the never-nevers?

Those years
when I heard only

mourning
in the *morning*.

Songs

Alvin Pleasant Carter was a man who knew—
a pilgrim of the ultimate tune.

A.P. at his counter,
hefting over the sacks of brown sugar—

years after the road, when he'd lost his Sara,
and a man can measure the weight of forever...

A.P. knew, stood in that general store,
we never hear the songs we are *listening for*.

The Cave

Cash—when he swore his life over.
This was Nickajack Cave in 1967,

as in *Cash* by Johnny Cash,
as told to Patrick Carr.

A classic of salvation. So what
if it never *actually* happened?

Ends make fiction of our means.
Johnny said it: he wasn't *lying*.

Difficult Ones
after W. S. Graham

Thirteen years, my difficult ones!
And what have I become?

This morning I set myself down
in the small room again,

its aspect on rain and time
being nothing if not instructive.

I contemplate water and glass.
What are you saying? I practise

in the ham tones of a lovers' silence,
which is all the same not loneliness—

not quite—my difficult ones,
since at the least absence

is a form of the lightness beginning.
Beautiful mutes,

how you crowd at the pane
of the mind— in each bead your faces

wild, your mouths the shape of
Not I! Not I!

Or so I am willed to imagine.
It is always April

on the tongue. Nothing is
begun again, yet something

cleaves or cleaves to sense.
My art is in the limerence.

Testament

O Brandon, my brown-eyed boy, I will not answer
critics who say you're a triumph of style over substance
and that your lyrics do not make grammatical sense.
I tell you now: I have known, myself, such an audience.
And when I listened to your solo effort, *Flamingo*,
I wept for that part of their heart that would not hear,
wept for that part of your heart that wept for them.
I was glad you maintained the talents of Stuart Price.

Brandon, in our early days, when first I Googled you
hourly, I will confess I feared you'd disappoint me
because you were too pretty. But then I read you were
a Mormon and, though you found it difficult, you rarely
took a drink or smoked a cigarette. There again,
I must admit the fact you had a wife to whom you are,
at present, faithful, and who is the mother of your three
children, dealt a blow of not inconsiderable proportion.

I cannot decide, Brandon, how I like you best, just as
you cannot decide how best you like yourself. There is,
for example, that latter Americana shot through
with a dash of Bryan Ferry. Or your neophyte's tribute
to Robert Smith of The Cure, which made me rethink
guyliner. And let us not forget your complex
relationship with facial hair, as mocked by Neil Tennant:
the baby-smooth, the bearded, or my sweet bandito.

When I read how you grew in the dust bowl of sin.
When I read how, by some coincidence the stars really
fixed for us, you listened in your room to The Cars
through the hell of your teenage years, you opened, softly,
the girl in me. Brandon, it is only by a twist of Bowie
on a stereo that you did not turn golf pro, these words are
written, and the film will not carry Charlize Theron
with her katana back into the white dot of oblivion.

And when I consider such things, such things.
Brandon, Brandon, even there, in your name, flowers.

The Adventurers

Out from the drives we join, one by one,
and do not ask where the grown-ups have
gone. Almost-spring is here again, lovely
against our cheeks in the evening air. We have
our sweaters on. We do not ask why
we are here—why tonight. The streamers
from my handlebars—so free, so light!
Look how big the moon is! someone shouts.
Everyone is out. Everyone is out from
the drives, even the kids who could never,
who could never waggle their way to
propulsion, whose mothers cared too much—
asthma or dietary problems or one cliché
after another serving as the explanation.
All are out, as the streetlamps tick and fizz.
We could fly! We could do anything!
Remember what it's like or never was?
Of course, there are the bad guys. Bad guys
are everywhere, out of sight, but they are
not us. And something—not good—
bleeds from a pipe on the edgelands.
Something long suspected by us, but missed
by the good, gone grown-ups. The bad guys
listen in the dark-windowed vans of the mind
you can't see. Now, we must speak softly.
We are out for treasure. We are out for trees,
and the big moon. A shy boy has a plan
and a map. We must be careful of the vans.
We have a boy with a plan. We came equipped
with torches, the requisite peanut butter-
and-jelly sandwiches. The bikes slip from our
grip. The bikes pile up. The shy boy puts
his finger to his lips. *Something is moving*,
he wants to say. Our round, credulous faces
burn and thin to the summation of meaning—
the beautiful horror, the mangled wonder.

Night Game

Lights in the stadium come on. The sound of God.
In retrospect, you think: everything was prescient.

Your friends and your enemies have taken their seats;
the air is live with hot dogs and beer.

Before you, in the Diamond Dust, lies the barrel
on which you burned: WONDERGIRL.

And the crowd wants what it wants, always louder,
and harder. Stepping up, at last, you see her—

pitching you all she's got—or ever had—
as if to prove that willow's rightful owner; but

you've failure enough to know there is no magic bat
outgames the sweet spot of the sheer, bloody *heart*.

'Beautiful berries'

Your fingers purpled—
the world for you

so peopled
hence thrawn

you would away
and they call it folly

even me
when I take this blueberry

and bite
no longer young

but learning now at last
something clearer

at once less clear
about the nature

of abundance
located in the nuance

it's true—I never hoofed
this world like you

but still I dreamed
and travelled far

all the same
so it would seem

this August evening
being

the forty-third of my life
my daughter

growing so softly
so softly

but determinedly
in her bedroom hourly

tangible now
what's giving way

losing so richly sweetly kindly
to the new

that's progress   Chris
that's purpose for you

I think
I guess

Yes—I could
I could

I could tell you now
about the nature

of abundance
but catch myself

there in time
each must find their own

beautiful
O beautiful berries

—
—
—
—
—
—

NOTES TO THE POEMS

Miramar
Intergenerational trauma, a flirtation with the Fair Unknown motif, beach volleyball, grief, redemption, self-actualisation, and one of the finest movie soundtracks of the 1980s... In lesser hands, *Top Gun* might well have become high art.

Six Ways of Looking at John Cazale
Cazale's brief but beautiful film career – over a seven-year, multi-Oscar-nomination period before his death from lung cancer aged just 42 – remains a masterclass in character acting.

A Bandana
Theories as to the multivalent purpose of DFW's signature bandana are explored by DT Max in *Every Love Story is a Ghost Story: A Life of David Foster Wallace.*

Shermerverse
This sequence pays affectionate tribute to characters and plots created by Hollywood's legendary auteur of 1980s teen angst, John Hughes (1950–2009). 'The Duckies, in their mid-life' references the changed ending of *Pretty in Pink* (1986) following negative test screenings.

As Told by Alan Smithee
'Alan Smithee': pseudonymous credit in use from 1969 to 2000, granted by the Directors Guild of America to unhappy film directors who were able to prove they had lost creative control of a project. Alan Smithee's extensive filmography includes such highlights as *The Barking Dog, Bloodsucking Pharaohs in Pittsburgh,* and *The Shrimp on the Barbie.*

The Portable Dorothy Parker
The strange, true story of Dorothy Parker's remains would – as likely as not – have greatly appealed to its mordant subject.

Hotel Cecil
Downtown L.A.'s erstwhile hotel of horrors.

I am the world's last barman poet and **Coughlin's Law #127**
'I am the world's last barman poet' takes as its starting point Brian Flanagan's declamation from the 1988 film *Cocktail,* written by Heywood

Gould and directed by Roger Donaldson. 'Coughlin's Law #127' is inspired by the acid wisdom of Flanagan's perennially cynical mentor, Doug Coughlin.

Bournemouth
My imagined meeting with the late, great poet Rosemary Tonks is proof that – even in the darkest hour – vanity dies hard.

Bruce the Shark
The collective nickname given by Steven Spielberg to the trio of frequently malfunctioning mechanical sharks deployed in *Jaws*.

Slightly, a Lost Boy
Roddy Lumsden (1966–2020).

Watermelons
Michael Donaghy (1954–2004).

Songs
Alvin Pleasant Carter: patriarch of the legendary Carter Family.

Night Game
'WONDERGIRL' reimagines Roy Hobbs's magic bat from Bernard Malamud's classic 1952 baseball novel, *The Natural*, and the 1984 film adaptation of the same name, starring Robert Redford. Much of my later life has amounted to a competitive sport with my younger self. I am probably not alone in this.

'Beautiful Berries'
Last written words of Chris McCandless, AKA Alexander Supertramp (1968–1992). The story of McCandless's ill-fated journey into Alaska – and into his self – is recorded in Jon Krakauer's *Into the Wild* and the film of the same name, directed by Sean Penn.

Acknowledgements

My thanks are due to the editors of the following publications in which some of these poems – or versions of them – first appeared: Nia Davies and Zoë Brigley at *Poetry Wales*, Gerry Cambridge at *The Dark Horse*, Naush Sabah at *Poetry Birmingham Literary Journal*, John McAuliffe at *The Manchester Review*, Jodie Hollander at *Poetry Quarterly*, Emily Trahair at *Planet: The Welsh Internationalist*, Tim Kindberg and Karen McCarthy Woolf at *Magma*, George Murray at *NewPoetry*, and W. N. Herbert and Andy Jackson at *New Boots and Pantisocracies*.

'Difficult Ones' was commissioned for *The Caught Habits of Language: An Entertainment for W.S. Graham for Him Having Reached Sixty-Five*, edited by Rachael Boast, Andy Ching, and Nathan Hamilton. Thank you for inviting me to the party, Rachael, Andy, and Nathan.

A small selection of poems first appeared in a limited-edition pamphlet, *Flowers*, which was published by Rack Press in 2017. My great gratitude to Nick and Sue Murray for making that experience a real joy.

I am enormously grateful for an individual artist's grant from Arts Council England, without which this book could not have been written.

To the wonderful Zoë Brigley, Rhian Edwards, and all at Seren for your wisdom and your belief in my journey to La La Land and back: I so appreciate your warmth and professionalism in all matters.

Love and thanks, always, to dear friends who possess a special talent for keeping me laughing during volatile times: Elizabeth Rees, Danielle Factor, Nathalie Carter, Celia Sabatini, Christian Hicks, Sinead Hemsley, Frank Hemsley, Rowena Vestey, Corin Vestey, Dan Whitcombe, Gerry Cambridge, Ann Wardle, Camellia Stafford, Geraldine Vincent, and Lucy Quarry. And a very heartfelt thank you to the wonderful Sarah Corbett, who told me to just get on with it. To lightly paraphrase Dorothy Parker: 'Constant use has not worn ragged the fabric of their friendship.'

Finally, to my most beloveds, Andrew and Eleanor Neilson: there's no place like home. Thank you, thank you—for everything.